SELF-DISCIPLINE 365

THE PATH TO FREEDOM AND ACHIEVEMENTS

RAPHAEL DUME

© *2020 by Raphael Dume*

All rights reserved. No part of this publication may be reproduced, distributed, or transmitted in any form or by any means, including photocopies, recordings, or other electronic or mechanical methods, without the prior written permission of the publisher, except in the case of brief citations incorporated in critical reviews and certain other non-commercial uses permitted by copyright law.

Library of Congress Control Number: 2020920594

ISBN: 9798698670278

Made in the United States of America

ALSO, BY RAPHAEL DUME

SELF-CONFIDENCE 101
SELF-CONFIDENCE 2.0
THE EFFECTIVE ART OF INFLUENCE PEOPLE
EDUCATED HABITS

Table of Contents

Preface 6
   Discipline: what is it about? 6

PART ONE 10
   Chapter One 10
      Procrastination 10

Chapter Two 24
   How to develop habits of great scope? 24
   How to create new habits 29

Chapter Three 40
   Prioritize 40

PARTTWO 56
   Chapter Four 56
   The power of staying focused 56

Chapter Five 61
   Master your brain 61

Chapter Six 79
   Clear your mind 79

Chapter Seven 94
   Six basic rituals for success 94

Conclusion..103
ABOUT THE AUTHOR......................................108

Preface

Discipline: what is it about?

Discipline is a pattern of conduct where you choose to do things you know you should do instead of those you want to do. Discipline is the inner power that pushes you to get out of bed to exercise, go to work, or do the housework every morning instead of sleeping for unnecessary hours. It is when you assert your willpower over the basic desires you have. Self-discipline is the synonym for success.

When you are disciplined, you have a personal initiative to start and finish regardless of resistance. If you are disciplined, you have the strength to endure difficulties, whether physical, mental, or emotional. This allows you to forgo immediate satisfaction in order to achieve something better, even if it takes time and effort.

Discipline is one of the cornerstones of living a fulfilling and successful life, something we must all master.

Once you are constantly doing the things you know you should do exactly at the time that you must do them, there are several benefits you will enjoy:

- Once you consistently do the things you know you need to do, you will also increase your chances of achieving your goals.

- People will respect you, including your spouse, your employees, and those around you that are able to see your efforts.

- Your self-esteem will shoot through the roof. Every time you push yourself to do things that you know you should do, your self-image will get stronger.

- You will influence the lives of others. All good and right things you do can influence the lives of others, and you may even have an effect of dominion over some of the future generations.

- You will witness greater success in the different facets of your life.

- Last but not least, your life will be more satisfying and rewarding when you are disciplined.

On the other side, if you're constantly neglecting the things you know you must do when you need to do them, there will be downsides you can expect:

- You will never be able to reach your targets.

- You will never feel good with yourself, even if you strive to justify your actions.

- You will lose the respect of the people who depend on your actions and those around you.

The choice of becoming a disciplined person can be considered one of the most crucial decisions you ever take in your life—this book will teach you how.

PART ONE

Chapter One

Procrastination

Procrastination is one of the biggest obstacles to achieving what you want out of life. Many of us have things that we want to achieve that we never accomplish. Too often, this is primarily due to the lack of a concentrated strategic effort.

Maybe you blame time—you could say that you would love to start your own business, improve your house, write a novel, clean the kitchen, but you just don't have time because you are so busy with work and taking care of your family. This is simply untrue.

We all have 24 hours in the day (16 of which we pass awake), and may not seem like much, but it should be more than enough to achieve everything you want. After all, didn't you see a whole box of your favorite TV show last month? Didn't you spend four hours a day playing the latest video game? Didn't you spend more than two hours watching TV and browsing Facebook on most nights of the past week? If you had spent all that time in a useful and productive way, then, of course, you would have achieved your goals—and probably much more. You probably would speak five languages now!

Part of the problem comes down to procrastination. But really this is the result of some much more important problems, those of energy and self-discipline. In this guide, you will learn how to solve *all* those problems.

Why you lack self-discipline?

Postponements stem from a lack of discipline. This is what happens when you sit down to work, and immediately, your mind begins to doubt. This, in terms, comes down to a couple of factors. For starters, the work you need to do is likely to be boring and unrewarding. If the job you had to do involved playing a computer game or eating a delicious cake, you probably wouldn't put it off.

The other problem comes down to stress and anxiety. When you feel anxious and stressed, your mind wants to turn to that source, but that stress does not allow you to get involved in the things you have to do. Therefore, you often find yourself killing time surfing the web –it's a bit like burying your heads in the sand and hoping the problem goes away. Of course, the irony is that the delay will only make things worse.

Ultimately, this is an example that you are not in control of your own mind. This is 'monkey mind.' This is a great example of how you can feel out of control when it comes to where you want to direct your energy. And that brings me to the other problem: *Energy*.

Often times, you are simply too tired to do what you need to do. Maybe you just had a long day at the office, and now you need to sort or clean the house. But you are too tired to do that, and therefore you think you should give yourself five minutes to rest first, which quickly turns into ten minutes or twenty, and then it's time to sleep.

Yeah, sometimes you lack energy and willpower to such an extent that you can postpone things until before the time of going to bed.

You find yourself watching junk TV or browsing Facebook when all you want to do is sleep because you can't cope with the thought of having to get up and brush your teeth and face your daily schedule. Energy is also responsible for this to a greater extent.

Self-discipline requires energy. Whenever you make a decision, right or wrong, it requires energy. This is why we also tend to become less moral as the day progresses. Our willpower is fatigued at this point, so we often take the easy route. Now that you know all this, the next question is how you can end procrastination and gain unstoppable willpower?

Why Self-discipline is so important

Willpower and discipline are actually two sides of the same coin, and this is an area of your life that you should seek to cultivate if you want to become a more impressive, powerful, and successful version of yourself. Ultimately, self-discipline comes down to controlling your own emotions and actions. And that, in turn, means that you must learn to stop being a *slave* to the way you feel. You don't want to work all night because it doesn't feel right. And so, you do it slowly, and your mind fights you every step of the way. However, a disciplined individual can simply tell himself that it doesn't matter if he likes it or not, it has to be done, and that's it. He chooses a goal, an objective, and excludes *all* other distracting thoughts and impulses.

This is a powerful thing because it allows you to get a laser focus on what you are doing and complete any task. Yet, at the same time, you also create consistency in everything you say and do. People will find that you are not easily annoyed by things that they can say or do. You will not be desperate to please others—You'll be determined, disciplined, and immune to the concerns of life.

This is *so* important. Many times, you try to please anyone because you want to be liked, you end up making weak decisions that end up annoying everyone. Very often, you let your emotions guide you in your conversations and disputes, which causes you to react badly. And very often, you curl up into a ball and don't do the things that need to be done, which only makes your life more difficult.

A disciplined person rises above this and has under control all his actions and reactions.

So how do you become that type of person?

How can you get unstoppable self-discipline?

How is discipline earned?

Self-discipline is earned in the same way you gain anything else—through practice and training. This also means that you need to recognize the discipline that exists in each moment all 365 days of the year. Discipline is the conscious choice to focus on one thing and avoid distractions. Distraction *is* procrastination, and procrastination is a distraction. So, when someone is speaking to you in a conversation, it's your job to focus on what this person is saying to you sharply. When you are supposed to be working in the office, but you are interested in whatever is happening on the other side of the office, it is your job to *ignore* this impulse. When you try to exercise, but you feel tired, it's your job to ignore the feeling and move on anyway.

Start by acknowledging that your feelings don't matter. As long as you don't get hurt, it doesn't matter if you're a little hungry, a little bored, a little cold, a little tired. It doesn't matter if you feel that you deserve a gift. Self-discipline is to resist those impulses and concentrate on things you should concentrate on to achieve your targets.

This type of training 'incidentally' converts all your interactions and experiences into opportunities to perfect your focus and discipline. But you can also create more training opportunities along with your routine.

An example might be taking a cold shower. Standing in a cold shower requires a great deal of willpower and self-discipline, and this is something that your body and mind will fight against every step of the way. But if you can force yourself to dive into that cold water anyway, you'll be training and harnessing your willpower. And indeed, cold showers are very good for you as it helps you to produce more testosterone, increase blood circulation, and train your immune system. Another example is making your bed. This is very simple, but it is a great habit to acquire—if you can motivate yourself and successfully make your bed every morning, even when you're stressed, even when in a hurry, then this will be a great workout for you to do *other* things you need.

The importance of the reward

It is important to be disciplined to fight procrastination, but *it is also* important to enjoy life. Moreover, no one will be disciplined 100% of the time, no matter what they tell you. Being too repressive and strict can end up leading to more serious problems down the road. Instead, what I'm saying is that you need to reward yourself along the way.

Do you want to eat a big chocolate bar? Sure, you can. But only once you've spent a whole day keeping your X number of calories. Do you want to relax and enjoy a good book? Great! But first, you need to complete X amount of work to have that under your belt.

Rewarding your good behavior is a great way to motivate yourself, allowing you to add some fun to your life *without* having to give up completely to be disciplined and strict.

A simple example of this would be your daily work. If you normally start your workday with a cup of tea and then chatting, it's time to turn that around. From now on, you get the cup of tea and the talk as a *reward* for doing another task. Only allow these things after you have completed X amount of work. This motivates and allows you to work with fewer interruptions. The same goes for checking your phone: Put it in silence and allow yourself to check it every hour for five minutes. Doing this helps prevent procrastination because your willpower will not be strong enough to avoid it *completely*. Instead, you just have to be strong enough to hold your impulse for a while.

One more thing...

One last thing you can do to get rid of Procrastination is: To meditate.

Meditation is an essential exercise in discipline. This is the practice of eliminating *all* thoughts that distracted you for a short period of time and, with this skill, you can start being *much* less easy to control by stress, fatigue, hunger, or other impulses. Meditation can make you much more disciplined, less stressed, and much better and able to focus and get focus for long periods of time—of course, that requires discipline. Start with small sessions of five minutes several times a week and go from there.

Exercise

What is the biggest obstacle to achieving what you want out of life?

Why do you lack self-discipline?

How can you get unstoppable self-discipline?

Why is self-discipline important for you? Mention one of the areas you would like to be more disciplined?

Chapter Two

How to develop habits of great scope?

Humans are creatures of habit. We have evolved over thousands of years so that we like routine, we like predictability, and we take root in a certain series of events.

Therefore, most of us have a routine that we follow practically every day. Maybe you start your day by waking up, taking a shower, getting dressed, making breakfast, and then watching the news for 10 minutes with a cup of coffee before running to your office.

You probably have a similar routine at night, which could involve making a purchase of 10 minutes in your local grocery store, cook dinner, watch TV, take a shower, and then reading a book in bed. You probably go to bed around the same time every day.

It's not by chance. This comes down to the whole way we are connected. The way our brain works and the way our biology works.

Repeating the same actions or thoughts over and over again essentially means that we are repeatedly using the same neural pathways and causing the same connections to fire and fire. As we do this, those connections become 'myelinated.'

That means they are isolated by myelin sheaths, so they get stronger and stronger. If you repeat one action followed by another often enough, they will often become so ingrained that they become automatic and beyond our conscious control.

This was perfectly demonstrated by the psychologist Ivan Pavlov, who managed to condition dogs to salivate to the sound of a bell.

This is also the reason why severely brain-damaged people who cannot remember their own names can still amazingly play the piano. Some can do this even without knowing that they can play the piano! The simple fact is that motor neurons are *scheduled* during years of practices. The groove has been oiled time and time again to leave a final impression.

As for our biology, it is completely based on rhythms and patterns. The sun rises at a certain time, and this triggers the release of cortisol and nitric oxide. These neurotransmitters trigger a cascade of activity throughout the brain that makes us more awake and active. Then we eat, and this slows us down a bit again and prepares us for work.

After the afternoon, our lunch settles in, and we start to get slower and slower thanks to a dose of melatonin and serotonin. By the time the sun begins to set, we are producing more melatonin, and the accumulation of adenosine in our brain makes it increasingly difficult to think.

If you wake up at a different time, if the sun rises at a different time, or if you eat a larger meal, this can throw the whole routine out of control and leave you in a bad mood as a result. This causes the lag time, which is why a solution to the jet lag involves altering mealtimes.

In short, the more we repeat the same behavior over and over, the more difficult it is for us to change that behavior.

If the behavior in question involves smoking, then this is bad news. But if the behavior involves going to the gym, then it's *great* news. For example, I have been reading at least 30 minutes a day since I was 16 years old (I will be 37 this year). That means I've been doing something constantly for almost 21 years. As expected, it is now almost impossible to stop. I love reading, it is part of who I am, and I do it without any effort.

In other words, harnessing the power of habit can be a powerful tool to help you get what you want out of life - a better body or a richer bank account.

The question is, how are you going to form those habits ...?

How to create new habits

The 30-day rule

You will often read that the best way to create a new habit is to repeat that action for thirty days. If you can do that, eventually, you will have ingrained the behavior deep enough that you cannot stop it. Is this true? Theoretically, thirty days would be enough to rehearse an action long enough for it to take hold.

Is this a magic number? It is very arbitrary. There is no reason why doing something for thirty days should be better than doing something for 29 or 31 days. While this idea has anecdotal evidence based on research, this appears to be accurate, and if you can develop a new behavior during this time, you're going to be at least on the right track.

This also makes getting started a bit easier. If you know that you need to exercise first thing in the morning for only thirty days, it may be easier to digest it than thinking that you need to do it permanently.

Micro habits

Are you having trouble flossing every day, even just for those 30 days? So, in that case, you might want to try using something called 'micro habits.' The idea of a micro habit is essential to hacking the 30-day trial by finding a way to maintain your habit during that time much easier and then extrapolating the results.

Micro habit means turning your planned new habit into something that is extremely easy and simple to accomplish. For example, your objective now could be to only floss *one* tooth and use thread dental tooth in a different one every night. There should be no difficulty in accomplishing it. But just like with a 'full-size' habit, you should find that this micro habit takes deep root after a while and that it will eventually become easy for you to stick with it. Now all you have to do is extend that habit to floss all your teeth!

A more realistic version of this could be if you wanted to write a novel, in which case you could aim to write just *one line* per night. In the same way, if you want to be fit, you can try to do only 20 push-ups every day.

This works best if what you're doing is still useful in its own right. For example, if you only did 20 push-ups, you would still notice some improvement. Similarly, writing just *one line per* night would *eventually* lead to a complete book.

Try to avoid a scenario where you can see and feel that your micro habit makes no sense.

The best thing about micro habits is that, early on, you'll find that sometimes you end up doing more. For example, if you've set a goal of doing 20 push-ups, you'll often find that you end up doing an entire workout either way – the hardest part is just getting started!

Most importantly, however, you have the *option* to use the micro habit by default. The important thing is that you keep this part of your routine, not as much as the habit itself (for now!).

Context

Another tip to create a new habit is to try to attach it to your old habits and environment.

In other words, if you want to create the habit of flossing, then a good option is to attach it to a habit that you are already us to like brushing your teeth.

In the same way, if you want to get in the habit of ironing your shirts, choose a specific point of the day, like making tea in the morning.

This works because it connects the new with the old behavior within your brain. You have a network of neurons that is activated every time you make your morning tea. Now when that network of neurons kicks in, they should also make the new network, the shirt press network turns on. The two are connected.

This also works on a practical level: You need to find a convenient time to develop your new habit, and you must find a convenient time and place to do it. Moreover, you should know that this time and place will always be convenient. You *always* need to be able to train right now, in this place.

For example, I wanted to start meditating as a regular part of my routine a while ago. I struggled at first because there always seemed to be more important things to do, and I could never find the right opportunity. So, what I did was attach my meditation session to my training session. I already was exercising 3 to 4 times a week, so all I did was include my meditation immediately after exercise. I meditate for just 5Minutes. That is a micro habit that would never take me too long, and I would always be in the right place to practice it.

Keeping an environment is important since everything in its periphery can help foster your habit. So, when trying to *break* a habit, the advice is always to change the environment immediately. If you're trying to quit alcohol or drugs, for example, one of the first things you need is to stop hanging out in the same places and with the same people. These have been associated with a habit, and they are now the ' triggers.' But if it's a *good* habit, triggers are a good thing!

The power of routine

An action is a habit, but if you join them, then you have a routine. I recently mentioned the practicality of joining habits and knowing where you will be and at what time it will be when you do it. This is incredibly important for achieving the goals and, if you can create a routine for you that contains *many* good habits, you will discover this greatly increases your chances of success in all areas.

For example, if you are starting a new training program, you should know exactly when you will exercise and where. If you simply say that you are going to train "five days a week," then this is not enough—you will put it off, and forget about it, or feel too tired.

Instead, look for a space on your routine where you can always have this space. For example, the best time for your training might be after you have left your wife at the station in the car. If you do this every morning and the gym is right next door, all you need to do is walk with everything you need to train.

The fact that you are already traveling means there is no extra time on the journey.

Similarly, if you want to eat a healthy diet, you need to identify when you are going to prepare your food and how you are going to eat it.

Creating a routine is a powerful *way to* achieve your objectives. But don't forget that the value of life comes from mixing things up and trying new things. Don't let yourself back down, or you'll start to atrophy and stop growing. Habits help you get where you want to go but don't forget to enjoy every moment.

Exercise

How does forming a routine can help you?

How does forming micro habits can help you in the long term?

How are your Habits affecting your life?

How can you use the 30-day rule?

Chapter Three

Prioritize

Everything in life cannot be a priority. Many important things will compete for attention over your lifetime, but there are not enough hours in anybody's lifetime to give attention to everything that could potentially be a priority.

Determining your basic priorities is a key exercise in moving toward more efficient use of your time. Your basic priorities provide a means for making time choices, helping you decide where it is important to invest your time and what you can let go of.

Prioritizing

Setting priorities is a matter of deciding what is especially important. In this case, "important" means significant to you. What activities and roles give meaning to your life, and are the components of your life where you would like to succeed the most?

You'll have to learn to set task priorities on your daily basics. Prioritizing tasks includes two steps:

- Recognizing what needs to be done
- Deciding on the order in which to do them

How do you determine what work needs to be done? For the most part, it relates back to your basic priorities. To be efficient in the use of your time, you have to weed out the work that does not fit within your basic priorities. Learn to say "no" to jobs that look interesting and may even provide a secure sense of accomplishment but do not fit with your basic priorities.

You also have to be able to separate out the tasks that require busywork that tends to eat away at your time. Many tasks that fill your day may not really need to be done at all or could be done less frequently. Task prioritizing means working on the most significant tasks first, regardless of how tempted you are to do the less significant tasks to just move it out of the way.

Certain skills help in using your time effectively. Most of these skills are mental. While it is not necessary to develop all the skills, each contributes to your ability to direct time usage.

Time sense is the skill of estimating how long a task will take to accomplish. A good sense of time will help you to be more realistic in planning your activities. It helps prevent the frustration of never having quite enough time to accomplish a particular task.

To increase your time sense, begin by making mental notes of how long it actually takes to do certain routine tasks like getting ready in the morning, running a load of laundry, or driving your child across town to a baseball practice.

Goal setting is the skill of deciding where you want to be at the end of a specific time. Goal setting gives direction to your morning, your day, your week, and your lifetime. The exercise on deciding your lifetime priorities is a form of goal setting. Learn to write down your goals.

If you are like most people, goals are just wishes until you write them down. Keep your goals specific, as in "weed the flower beds in front of the house" rather than "work on the yard." Keep your goals realistic, or you will continually be frustrated by a sense of failure.

Adjust your standards as circumstances change. Your standards are what you use to judge whether something is good enough, clean enough, pretty enough, done well enough.

Perfectionists have extremely high, rigid standards, and they have trouble adjusting to the changing demands or circumstances of their life. Develop the ability to shift standards so you can be satisfied with less than perfect when your time demands are high, instead of feeling as if you are somehow falling short.

Time planning is outlining ahead of time the work you need to be done in a specific period. Sometimes, time planning is as simple as writing a to-do list to ease your mind from holding on to too much detail.

At particularly stressful times, a "To Do List" may expand to include a more specific calendar of when tasks will be done. While a detailed time schedule can be too confining to use all the time— it is a good way to take the pressure off at exceptionally demanding times.

Recognizing procrastination is a skill because procrastinators can do an incredible job of hiding their procrastination from themselves.

You might disguise the procrastination response with an excuse like waiting for inspiration or needing a large block of time to concentrate with your full attention, or needing more information before tackling a project.

It takes skill to differentiate between procrastination excuses and legitimate reasons for delaying a decision or action. Without the ability to recognize when you are procrastinating, there is little chance of overcoming this immobilizing habit.

Techniques you can use to prioritize

You can use these tips on a regular basis to remain focused. Each of these techniques can help you in getting closer to your goal of becoming more effective with your time.

1. Assume ownership of your time

Most individuals would be surprised if somebody reached in their wallet without asking and helped themselves to the money found there. But how different is that from letting other people help themselves with your time? Take possession of your own time and do not allow other people to make commitments of your time without your permission. It is not selfish to keep others from consuming your time. Give your time freely when you want but do not make the mistake of undervaluing this resource—or feeling guilty when you do not allow others to waste it. Think of a time lately when somebody wasted your time. How could you have dealt with the situation better?

2. Prioritize

Continually check yourself to see that you're working on the most significant things. Helping your child with a math problem or discussing the day's events with your spouse or friend may be more significant than getting the dishes done or complete a load of laundry. Do not think of priorities only as tasks that need to be done. As you remind yourself to direct yourself to the most important tasks first, you will find yourself letting go of tasks that really did not need to be done in the first place.

3. Learn to say "no."

It is not that saying the word "NO" is difficult, but it is more the feeling of guilt that many people experience as soon as they use the word. Try centering on the significant things that will be done because you used that two-letter word to decline something which was not a part of your priorities. Considering your past week, what are some things you should have said "no" to?

4. Protect your blocks

Think of your day as numerous large blocks of time with the blocks divided by natural interruptions where you have control to keep your blocks whole, scheduling appointments and meetings, running errands at the beginning or end of a block instead of in the middle. Having an appointment in the middle of a block leaves little time at either end to tackle a major piece of work. Keeping your blocks of time as big as possible gives you the feeling of having more time available.

5. Delegate

Delegating means assigning the responsibility for a task to somebody else. That signifies you no longer have to do the task, nor do you have to remind somebody else to do it. Being able to delegate some tasks is a way of freeing up some of your time for the jobs that only you can do. As somebody else learns to do a job, do not be tempted to take over if they are not doing it quite right. You must learn to exercise patience and train them better.

6. Learn to buy time

There is an intimate relationship between time and money, where one can often be substituted for the other. The more hectic your schedule, the more reasonable it is to buy time by selecting goods and services that save you from investing time. Paying somebody to mow your yard or drive your kid to a baseball practice are examples of buying time. What are some of the tasks you are doing that you can buy some time?

7. Learn to work with your biological clock

People have a peak time of day when their energy is at their highest and concentration at their best. Determine which time of the day is your peak performance time and plan your work accordingly. Keep meetings and routine tasks for other parts of the day when you have the choice. What part of the day is best for you to do a task that takes real concentration?

8. Break down big jobs into manageable pieces

One of the sources of procrastination is that some tasks can seem too overwhelming to start. Learn to break down a large task into manageable pieces and then begin with a piece you know you can handle. The most challenging step in major undertakings is often the first one. Besides, you will have a greater sense of satisfaction as you complete each individual portion of the task, and this can keep you motivated to the end. Think of a major task you have ahead of you.

How could you break it down into manageable pieces?

9. Work on overcoming procrastination

Once you recognize that you are procrastinating, the next step is to begin overcoming this time-wasting habit. Procrastination is a habit— a habitual way of dealing with tasks you find distasteful or that make you fearful of failure. When you see that you are procrastinating, make an appointment with yourself to take the first step toward completing the task. Determine exactly what that first step will be and then set a specific time soon to begin the work.

10. Reward yourself

Celebrate when a major task is completed or a major challenge is met. One of the problems with a hectic life is that you can be so busy that you fail to notice the completion of a major piece of work. You just move on to the next job without celebrating your previous success. This failure leads to focusing on what is still left undone instead of enjoying what has already been accomplished. Set up a reward system for yourself that serves as both a motivator to get certain difficult tasks done and an acknowledgment that you are making effective use of your time.

Exercise

How does prioritizing your basics tasks can help you?

How can delegating help you to achieve your goals?

Why is it important to reward yourself after a major accomplishment?

Which tasks aren't useful in your life that you can stop doing them today?

PART TWO

Chapter Four

The power of staying focused

You might say it is because you don't have the willpower to accomplish what you set out to do. You might say it is because you are too busy or too overwhelmed to act on your resolution. My guess is, it could be any of those things, but it is more likely that you have just started down a path without your compass, and you have started to lose your way.

Rather than rattling off a list of things, sit down and think about what you really want to achieve and set a solid intention to accomplish your goal. I also suggest that you focus on only one or two intentions at a time. No matter what you would like to achieve, setting an intention can and will set you on a course for success.

Here are 5 top tips to finally achieve your goal:

1- Get clear. In setting an intention, you're making it clear to yourself and to others exactly what you plan to do. Define the definition of what accomplishing your goal would be. For instance, you know you've reached your goal of improving your management skills when you consistently feel more satisfied with your ability to deal with tough situations and motivate your staff. You may even get that promotion you have been after!

2- Realize that an intention comes in several sizes, and every large goal is filled with big and small intentions. With follow-through, each intention will ultimately lead to success. For instance, if your resolution is to improve your management skills, your first intention may be to speak with your upper managers to find out what skills and traits you may want to focus on.

3-Do not let confusion overwhelm your intention. You may have lots of passion for your resolution, but passion without a plan is wasted energy and will eventually fizzle out. Setting an intention to take a step towards your goal each day will keep you on the right path and help to clear away confusion.

4- Use your resources. Ask for what you want and need from other people. For instance, if you look up to somebody's management style, ask him or her for tips, and possibly even support. Chances are they will be flattered and very willing to share advice.

5- Be accountable. Choose your resolutions carefully by deciding what really interests you and take responsibility even when things don't work as it should. Don't make excuses, and don't throw others under the bus. Nevertheless, nothing can take the place of honoring your intentions to yourself. You will be amazed at how your self-esteem and sense of accomplishment will increase when you hold yourself accountable.

Exercise

Do you hold yourself accountable without making excuses and without blaming others?

Why focusing on your goals is key?

Why do you need to be clear on your objectives?

How can you be more focused?

Chapter Five

Master your brain

If you were to buy a car, a computer, a game console, or even a toy of some kind, then in all probability, it would come with an instruction manual of some kind, so that you can figure out how to use it. This is important because it allows you to get the most out of it and allows you to avoid making mistakes that could damage it.

But unfortunately, the most important and complex things in the world come without an instruction manual. Take children, for example, any new parents will tell you how shocked they were when they realized that no one could tell them how to be an effective parent.

And then there's the biggest one: Our own brain. These are the most complex supercomputers in the entire world, and they are the ones that create all of our subjective feelings, sensations, and experiences. And yet our brains come without instructions or guidance.

So, the question is, how can you master your brain?

Fortunately, neuroscientists and psychologists are discovering more secrets of the brain every day. Although there is still a *huge* amount to learn, we know more about ourselves, and much of this information can be used to help us become happier, smarter, and more effective versions of ourselves.

How your brain works

Neuroscience is a subject that can take decades to learn, and even then, it will be necessary to specialize in one area; as I said, it is a complex piece of machinery. So, there is much more than can be explained here, but nonetheless, I am going to give you a brief overview so that you have a basic understanding of some important clues on how the brain *essentially* works.

So, what do we know?

First, the brain is made up of neurons. These neurons are cells that have long tendrils called axons and dendrites. These extend almost to touch each other, and that, in turn, means that they will be close enough for small signals to jump through space. This, in turn, creates a huge map made up of billions of neurons with incredibly intricate connections. This network is called the 'connectome,' and it is slightly different for everyone. These individual differences are what give us our different abilities and our different personalities. Each experience you have can be assigned to one or more of these neurons. Each neuron represents a sensation, a memory, an experience, a feeling, or something else. His vision is assigned to a wide variety of neurons that represent what you are seeing, and, in the same way, your memory consists of many interconnected neurons that reflect your thoughts and ideas.

These neurons are grouped around different regions of the function of your brain. In the occipital lobe, for example, we have all the neurons responsible for our sight. In the motor cortex, we have neurons that correspond to movements and sensations throughout our bodies. Our prefrontal cortex is where we handle things like planning and motivation. Our brainstem handles respiration. And our hippocampus stores many of our memories. This is why damage to a specific area of the brain can result in the loss of a specific function, and this organization is so extreme that there have even been cases in which a head injury has led a patient to lose the memory of vegetables and *nothing else.*

Interactions between neurons occur through "action potentials." These are electrical impulses that occur once a neuron has received sufficient stimulation. That stimulation is usually the result of many nearby neurons firing enough to overcome a certain threshold of excitability. When an action potential occurs, this can also result in the release of neurotransmitters. These are chemicals released by vesicles (sacs) that alter the way neurons function, perhaps making them prone to skyrocket, or perhaps making the event seem important, sad, happy, or memorable.

Another factor that influences our individual differences is our balance of neurotransmitters and hormones. If you have a lot of the feel-good neurotransmitter serotonin, you will often be in a good mood and relaxed. If you have a lot of cortisol and glutamate, then you will be a more connected and panicky person.

Neurotransmitters and external influences

What is important to recognize here is that the neurotransmitters are not *only the* result of what happens in the brain but can also be the result of biological signals of our body. For example, if you have a low sugar level in the blood, then your brain produces more cortisol, the stress hormone. This is an evolutionary response that is meant to make us look for more food, but it's also why we tend to feel anxious and angry when we haven't eaten for a while. This is where the experience of being 'hungry' comes from.

On the contrary, serotonin can be released when we eat something, and our blood sugar level rises. This makes us feel good when we finished eating. However, that serotonin is eventually converted to melatonin, which is the neurotransmitter for sleep that suppresses neuronal activity. This is why we often feel tired and groggy after a big meal.

Countless other things also influence our balance of brain chemicals. Bright light, for example, can reduce the production of melatonin and increase the production of cortisol and nitric oxide to wake us up. Remember: There were no artificial lights in nature, so our brain could rely solely on this signal to know what time it was.

While there is much more to it than that, it generally describes the shape and function of the brain and how it gives rise to our individual experiences.

Brain plasticity

Another aspect of the brain that is especially important to become familiar with is plasticity. Brain plasticity, also called neuroplasticity, is the brain's ability to adapt and grow.

For a long time, it was thought that the brain *only* formed new neurons and connections during childhood, and from then on, it was set in stone. However, we now know that this process continues until we die and is a crucial aspect of how our brain works. It slows down slightly in adults, but it is still what gives us the ability to learn, change our minds, and acquire new skills.

Neural plasticity occurs through practice, repetition, and events that we believe are especially important. The saying among neuroscientists goes thus: "What lights up together, connects together." In other words, if you experience something, a neuron will fire. If you experience that thing at the same time as another, it is possible that *two* neurons (or more likely, two groups of thousands of neurons) fire.

If you keep re-experiencing those two things together, a connection will begin to form between them. Later, that connection will be strengthened through a process called myelination, during which dendrites and axons isolate themselves to better conduct the flow of electricity. Eventually, a firing neuron will *cause* the other neuron to fire. This is how you can learn a complex series of movements when performing a dance or how you can remember words in a new language.

So how do you hack your brain and take control of your performance?

This may seem a lot to learn, but hopefully, you learned the basics with respect to various functions of your brain. Hopefully, you may have found some of this quite interesting as well. After all, it is *relevant* to all of us!

So now, the question is, how can you use this information productively?

Neurotransmitter control

One way to hack your brain to achieve higher productivity, happiness, or anything else is to influence neurotransmitter production—
these influence our mood and our ability to learn. Therefore, many people are interested in the idea of nootropics. The nootropics are smart drugs: supplements and medications that may influence the production of the neurotransmitters dopamine, so we have goal-oriented cortisol inducing fear. Modafinil alters the production of orexin, which can completely change our cycle of sleep, wakefulness, so we feel more awake most of the time. This is also what caffeine does, by removing the inhibitory

neurotransmitter adenosine (or neutralizing it, to be more precise).

The problem with this strategy is that it sets the brain on a specific and unnatural state and prevents you from being able to easily change your mode. No brain state is superior to all others. For example, creativity requires relaxation, not stimulation. Worse still, the brain can adapt to these changes by creating more or less "receptor sites" (the points where neurotransmitters work) to make us sensitive to the neurotransmitters in question. This can eventually lead to addiction. Some neurotransmitters work better by focusing more on neuroplasticity or more on energy production, but for the most part, this is *not* the solution.

What is a much more useful solution is to look at those factors that naturally influence the release of neurotransmitters? If you want to hack any system, the answer is to look at what the inputs are.

So, we know that bright light can boost energy and make us less sleepy, so why not consider investing in a daylight lamp designed to combat SAD (seasonal affective disorder) by simulating the rays of the sun. We know that cold can also increase concentration, while heat can help us feel more relaxed and happier. We know that the sun and exercise can improve our mood by producing serotonin.

We also know that our brains are subject to certain natural cycles related to sleep and hunger. For example, by timing our productivity *around* those things, we can work more efficiently and free from distractions.

And if you feel incredibly stressed or depressed, then it might be useful to consider some of the biological factors that may be causing that. Maybe you are hungry? Or maybe you're a little sick, and the pro-inflammatory cytokines are causing mental confusion? Once you know that the problem is temporary and biological, it can be much easier to let it go.

Most importantly, however, it is critical that you learn to create the moods and feelings you need by changing the way you think and use your brain.

What makes humans unique is our ability to visualize, internalize events, and imagine future scenarios or possibilities. This is our working memory at stake, and it is what allows us to think about long-term goals and invent new ideas. And if you believe in the theory of 'built-in cognition,' you might find that this is even what we use to understand plain English.

When we visualize or imagine, we do so by lighting up the same neurons in the brain as if the event were actually happening. Neurologically, we find ourselves doing something and imagining, doing something almost indistinguishable.

This means that you can use visualization to practice things and develop skills; You can activate brain plasticity as if you were practicing the event! But not only that, you can also use this as a way to activate the right neurotransmitters to put yourself in the right state of mind.

Ultimately this will lead to the ability to control your own emotions to activate the best possible state of mind for the task at hand. It requires training your visualization skills and awareness, and then *using* those skills to ease your anxiety and motivate yourself to focus and be more alert as needed. This is the neuroscience that underlies psychological approaches like cognitive behavioral therapy and philosophies like Stoicism.

This is *also* why it is so important to avoid bad habits, even bad habits in our thoughts, as reflecting and indulging strengthens the connections that make those habits increasingly difficult to break.

There is much more to getting the most out of your own brain, but I hope this primer has given you a better understanding and a little more control.

Exercise

How can you alter your brain?

In which ways can you use neurotransmitters?

Until what age can humans still form new neurons?

How can you combat SAD?

Chapter Six

Clear your mind

All your experience and quality of life depends on your ability to clear and control your mind.

Many of us believe that our happiness and most things that happen to us depends on external factors. This, however, is not true. Our happiness depends on the way we *react* to what happens to us. And so, does every other aspect of our experience: Our stress levels result from the way we react to events, and our ability to be productive also depends on our reactions.

Let's imagine you are in a caravan and is hanging over the edge of a cliff. If you move too much, you will fall off the edge into a ravine. If you are aware of this situation, it is likely that you feel fraught with fear. Your heart rate will increase, your blood vessels will dilate, your muscles will shrink, and you will begin to breathe rapidly. You'll be sweating, and your mind will be all over the place.

But now let's imagine that you are in the *same* situation, but *you think* you can fly. In that case, you are probably happy to read and not worry too much about all your precarious position.

As you can see here, your belief about the situation and events is what is in controls, not your mood, but also your physiology. And guess which person is most likely to survive this situation without dropping the caravan?

You must not convince yourself that you can fly.

But this is simply a demonstration of the power of the mind and your beliefs. Now, if you imagine yourself in a more realistic scenario, you can see how your beliefs can change the way you react.

Let's say you are standing on stage, and you are about to give a speech in front of a lot of people.

Some of us don't believe we can fly. Some of us think that we are going to say the wrong thing, that we are going to stutter, and that people are going to laugh at us. So, we start to panic, and guess what? Our blood vessels dilate, our muscles contract, and our heart rate goes up. Our mind starts racing, which makes us *more prone* to making mistakes, and our throat becomes dry and hoarse. The irony is that the speech is much more likely to go wrong simply because we are concerned that the speech will go wrong.

And now imagine the same scenario, but in which you think that everything will be fine, or in which you don't worry about what other people might think. This kind of quiet attention will help you act like there's not even an audience there!

Again, it is your reaction to the event that is going to keep stress at bay.

However, it's not just these highly stressful situations that can also benefit from mindfulness and calm. Imagine, for example, that you come home from work and cannot stop thinking about the last thing your boss, client, or colleague said to you. So, you wonder if you sent that important last email ...

How present will you be when you get home? How likely is that your family will enjoy spending time with you?

Imagine that you are on vacation, but the only thing you can think about is whether or not you left the oven on at home. How much do you think you will enjoy the incredible views of the mountains that pass through your window?

Imagine that you are in the gym and your mind is thinking about the computer game you were playing last night, or X Factor. Do you really think that you will be able to exert maximum force in that training?

Introduction to CBT

My goal is to help you regain control of your mind and, at the same time, also regain control over your emotions, feelings, and total discipline.

The end result is that you're going to be able to become completely present in any given moment and completely mindful, thereby abandoning unhelpful concerns, stressors, and emotions. CBT means 'Cognitive Behavioral Therapy' and is about to take control of your thoughts. CBT begins using a form of mindfulness meditation.

Mindfulness meditation means that you are meditating in such a way that you become more aware of your own thoughts and feelings. In other forms of meditation, such as transcendental meditation, ask the user to try to completely clear their mind, often focusing on a single point in space, or perhaps on a sound or word (this is called a 'mantra' and is why do we imagine Buddhist monks humming while meditating!). The difference with mindfulness is that you are not trying to eradicate your thoughts, but you are simply trying to 'watch' them as they float passing you. The idea is that you realize the kinds of things that you normally think about, but you are not committing to them, and you are not allowing them to affect you. The description is often that you must see them pass "like clouds in the sky."

Do this for a while, and then write down the content of some of those thoughts. Observe the things that stress and worry you on a regular basis and reflect on them in an objective and disconnected way, without judgment.

Start by analyzing those thoughts. Some of these will be things that you are going to be worrying and stressing about and which are going to stop you from enjoying yourself in the present moment. You are going to practice discarding them, but to help you, you are also going to take them apart using restructuring techniques.

An example of this is called "challenge of thought," which teaches you to challenge the validity of your concerns or distractions.

For example, let's say you are worried about not having sent an email at your job. You can overcome this by challenge your thinking. First, you wonder if there is anything you can do about it. If not, what good is worrying about it? In fact, it is more important that you relax and enjoy yourself so that you can be fresh and well to face the challenges of tomorrow.

Next, ask how much it really matters. What is the worst case? Most of the time, we worry about insignificant small little things. We all make mistakes. It is better to spend time explaining the mistakes than worrying about it.

How to use body scan meditation

In general, meditation is one of the most important ways to promote mindfulness, calm, and self-control.

In the book *Tools of Titans,* Tim Ferriss look s at the habits and routines of the world's most successful people. What he discovers is that all have many things in common, and one of the points in common *frequently* is that all of them meditate! Everyone from Arnold Schwarzenegger to Tony Robbins to Elon Musk describes meditation as a key tool that helped them achieve everything they have done.

When you learn to meditate, you start a method to forget your worries. However, the most important thing is that you develop a greater concentration and more focus, preventing your mind from finding an anxious mess to begin with.

So how do you start meditating?

One useful strategy is to start with the body scan technique. To begin, sit in a comfortable place with your legs crossed and your hands on your knees. Keep your back straight, chin up and forward, eyes closed, but make sure you aren't in a position where you can fall asleep.

Now you're going to simply scan your body by focusing on each part one at a time and then making a note of how it feels and relaxing it. Listen carefully to the world around you. You will find that there are sounds that you have completely blocked out until now, and you'll notice birds tweeting, cars honking, children playing, and the wind howling.

Feel the temperature of your skin, notice if you're on a slight gradient and even look at the light as it dances through your eyelids.

Okay, now focus on the top of your head and start to take your attention down to your cheeks, jaw, and then neck and shoulders. Stop at each point and make a note of how it feels: Are you carrying any tension? Are you feeling any pain? Release tension in the muscle and then keep moving.

Eventually, you'll reach the very bottom of your body. At which point, you can begin to concentrate on your breathing for a while.

Breathing should be 'belly breathing,' which begins with the gut expanding and then fills the lungs all the way up. Breathing steadily and rhythmically will slow the heart rate via the parasympathetic nervous system and put you in an even calmer state. Finally, bring your attention to just below the navel and hold it there. This is your center of gravity and concentrating here will ground you.

Throughout this process, you might notice your thoughts start to

drift from time to time. If this happens, don't let it concern you. It is normal and not the end of the world—just quietly dismiss those thoughts and then return to the focus.

Finally, repeat the steps in reverse order and bring yourself back around. That was a body scan meditation!

This is a powerful tool because it is forcing you to direct your attention and to ignore the outside thoughts. More importantly, it is engaging you with your own body, physicality, and surroundings. And when you do this, your sensations become richer and more vivid.

Eventually, if you keep practicing this skill, you should get to the point where you can begin to become more mindful and more present—even while moving and engaging in other tasks. That means just taking a moment to look at the world around you, pausing to see what you can hear, and fixing your posture. It means not getting so caught up in your own thoughts that you let life pass you by, or that you live in a constant state of stress and anxiety.

Once you can do this, then you will find that nothing can stir you up the same way unless you want it to. You can always just enjoy being in the moment and forget the past and the future for a time. You can enjoy living and taste the amazing taste of that chocolate biscuit while that email sits there in your outbox completely unsent.

This is the key to happiness— you can *choose* to react positively instead of negatively. You can choose to view things as a challenge or an amusing hiccup instead of a serious threat. But it is also the key to unlocking your full potential, so you perform better and achieve more.

Exercise

What are the benefits of having a clear mind?

How can you use CBT to be more discipline?

Did you practice scan meditation? How did you feel?

How can the "challenge of thoughts" may help you?

Chapter Seven

Six basic rituals for success

There are six core areas of success. Each area is important to create balance in your life. If you ignore one of the six main areas of success, you will not be able to function at your best. You have a sense of lack in your life and could even waste time trying to fill the void with the wrong things.

The six main areas of success:

1. Physical Health: It is important to make sure to do everything possible to keep physical health at all costs. It is quite logical that one of two things happen if you do not keep a healthy body and mind. You will have to spend a fortune on medicines and doctors, or it will lead to an untimely death due to some kind of health problem. Exercising, eating healthy, getting enough sleep, and drinking plenty of water can help you keep you healthy.

2. Emotions: Your emotions affect your mind. If you are mentally ill or unstable, then you cannot make objective decisions. A decision made when you are emotionally unstable can wreak havoc on your life.

The six core areas of success are correlated. Take, for example, if something happens that triggers your negative emotions (you may be feeling sad or angry), you can always exercise to calm yourself. It is not only your negative emotions that you must learn to control because if you are too excited or happy, you can also make the wrong decision. For example, if you are overzealous, you could spend money on things you do not need, and that money could be so invested in something that increases your income and quality of life. Life is about creating the right balance in everything you do.

3. Relationships: Your relations can affect your health and emotions. A toxic relationship will leave you with feelings of despair and anger. Unhappiness and anger can lead to depression. Depression affects your progress, either losing time to work or making decisions, which ultimately will result in failure.

The benefit of good relationships will create a paradise for you on earth. The world in your eyes is at peace because your heart is full of love, and your mind will have its cover made of thoughts of joy. You will work better. You will be more eager to get up in the morning because you are grateful for another day to be with your loved ones.

Examine your relationships and see how they are affecting your life. If you have been around someone who makes you feel overwhelmed, or you feel like that person is taking away all your hope and joy, then that is a toxic connection. You need to disconnect from that person. Relationships that motivate you to improve or those that help your ideas shine are what you need in your life.

4. Career or Business: Observe the attitude shown by people in your workplace, and this can always tell who loves his job and who does not. If you are not in a job, career, or business that makes you feel that this is what you were born to do, then you might be in the wrong field. Your career or business must make you satisfied no matter what obstacles you face daily. When in the right field, it will be easier to stay focused and, because of the passion you feel for your career or business, failure cannot convince you to quit.

5. Finance:

Rich and happy is the wish of all of us. However, if you want to be rich, it might take years of hard work to do it but, it can only take a minute of a bad investment, which will result in losing all of your money. If you do not have money, it is possible that you feel unhappy because you cannot buy the things you need to keep you and your family comfortable. Not having money can also prevent you from invest in your career or business. However, you can have money and still not be happy because there is an imbalance in one of the other five core areas of success. Never spend money on things just because you want to impress others. It is definitely not a ritual of successful people. The richest people alive are humble, and some of them say they don't need much to live happily.

For example, Bill Gates has topped several billionaire lists for years, and Bill Gates has been known to sit comfortably in economy class on airplanes when traveling.

Warren Buffet, with all his billions, is very happy in his house, which he bought for less than $40,000 many years ago. He also continues to discuss the multi-billion-dollar transaction on his foldable phone, which he has not replaced by any of the high-tech cell phones that are available today.

They return a portion of their wealth to various charities. Sometimes it is a charity they have started or one that is already in operation. Even after death, the richest people share their fortune. Many wealthy people are willing to participate in charities. Melinda Gates and Bill Gates have a grant-making foundation where they donate billions to different charities around the world. They have also encouraged other billionaires to donate part of their fortunes to the less fortunate and to combat diseases.

You should also adopt this principle of giving back to the less fortunate. Just as you will begin to practice the other rituals of success, this is a habit that you must also develop. Give as much as you can to charity now, and as your wealth increases, so does the portion for charity.

6. Spirituality: No matter what your religious preference is, spirituality is an important aspect of spiritual success. Spirituality can be found all around you, from time spent in nature to meditation and your religious practices. Spirituality has the ability to land you and keep you close to your own personal feelings and help you overcome anxiety and excitement, which allows you to make clear judgments.

Conclusion

Do not give up on your dreams. Maybe it can take you more time than you had planned to reach your objectives, but with the power embedded in your mind, you can conquer the world one day at a time. Never let procrastination stall your progress. Don't let failure stop you—learn any lessons arising from one failure and restart your trip.

The more you use your skills, the more you'll discover other hidden treasures of skills that were buried in you. I can guarantee you that you'll be amazed at the things you can do. Your talent can take you to places you never even imagined. The hard work and sacrifices you make to succeed will pay off. In fact, on your journey to success, every overcome challenge will become a distant memory because the rewards will outweigh the struggles.

Be reminded that success is a lifestyle, one in which after tasted is very addictive. I may not know your name or where you are from. I may not know what you've been through or what you're going through right now. However, I know that you have something inside of you, something that sets you apart from the rest of the people in your line of work. You need to find that part of your skill because it is your key to the door of success. No one in the world can do it for you, this is something you must do on your own.

I believe that you bought this book because that key, which is a part of your skill, has been nudging you. It's telling you that you can do this; you have what it takes. Do not be afraid. All it takes are some small steps, and the small steps will one day be an exceptionally long journey, a journey of no regrets because you tried and had achieved.

Everything in life is a choice; the only thing we can't choose about is when we'll die.

If you have created doubts at this moment, thinking that you do not have the money to invest in your plans, then the money is not preventing you from achieving your goals, but you are only preventing yourself from progressing. Observe your inner thoughts, and they will influence what you do. Speak positive words to yourself every day. You will have many options, but you will never decide to stop. Promise yourself that you will not stop, no matter how bad things get.

Work on your self-education; it is a powerful tool. Use technology. Establish a connection with people who succeed in your field, sell your plans. Describe your goals with such passion that they have to listen to.

Prepare for the "No" is only part of your learning experience. Do not be angry with those who reject your plan. You cannot blame them for not understanding the greatness within you. Most people who will say no now someday will beg you to be part of your projects.

Keep your spirituality firm—you can connect to the earth. It will give you clarity and motivate you to understand your inner self and to find your place in the universe. Spirituality doesn't have to be religious. Spirituality is a state of consciousness that allows you to specify your wishes for the future with a clear mind and a relaxed body.

Thank you for reading this book, and I hope to see you at the top. I wish you well on your journey to success!

ABOUT THE AUTHOR

Raphael Dume is an American author and internet entrepreneur who helps and inspires thousands of people to smash their goals and achieve the very best of their potential. His self-help books have been proven to improve self-esteem, resilience, happiness, optimism, and curiosity while reducing symptoms of depression, anxiety, and anger.

He focuses on helping others by documenting his personal learning and experiences through his writings. He shares his works that are easy to understand and strategies that can be easily applied in everyone's day to day life. He currently lives in New Jersey with his family.

www.ingramcontent.com/pod-product-compliance
Lightning Source LLC
Chambersburg PA
CBHW020443220526
45464CB00002B/835